21 Prayers of Faith

Overcoming Fear and Doubt Through the Power of Prayer and God's Word

Shelley Hitz

21 Prayers of Faith
© 2014 Body and Soul Publishing

Published by Body and Soul Publishing
Printed In The United States Of America

ISBN-13: 978-1-946118-12-7

CONTENTS

21 Prayers of Faith
Introduction

Prayer changes things. It changes me. When I pray consistently to God something changes within me. However, sometimes it is easy to get caught up in the busyness of life and not take the time to pray.

We do not have to pray in a certain way for God to hear us. We can simply lift up the prayer of our hearts to Him as if we are talking with a friend. However, in this book, I have used examples of faith found in scripture and reworded them into prayers. Combining prayer with God's Word is powerful. I have experienced this in my own life and now want to share it with you.

They say it takes 21 days to form a new habit. And so I have shared 21 prayers of faith with you to help you form a habit of prayer in your life. I pray that these prayers help you to overcome fear and doubt by applying the power of prayer and God's Word to your life. I also pray that when you finish this book, your prayers will continue on your own. I encourage you to dig into God's Word and come up with your own prayers. If you are struggling in a certain area, I recommend using a concordance or an online tool like BibleGateway.com or BlueLetterBible.org to find scriptures on that topic and then reword them into prayers from your own heart.

Are you ready to get started? Let's start with a prayer...

Lord, I thank You for each person who reads this book and lifts up these prayers to You. I pray that You would do a mighty work in their hearts as they spend these next 21 days in prayer with You. Change them from the inside out through Your Word and prayer. Give them a hunger and thirst for You that will continue past the last page of this book. We love You and thank You for this opportunity to come to You with our prayers of faith. Amen.

"Pray without ceasing."
- I Thessalonians 5:17 (NKJV)

"Ask, and it will be given to you; seek, and you will find; knock, and it will be opened to you."
- Matthew 7:7 (NKJV)

"Be anxious for nothing, but in everything by prayer and supplication, with thanksgiving, let Your requests be made known to God; and the peace of God, which surpasses all understanding, will guard Your hearts and minds through Christ Jesus."
- Philippians 4:6-7 (NKJV)

Prayer of Faith #1:
NOAH

Lord, I need You today. There are things in my life that just don't make sense. Help me to trust You even when I don't understand all the details or see how everything will turn out.

This reminds me of Noah and how You asked him to build an ark. You asked him to do something that did not make sense. His friends must have thought he was crazy for building a giant boat when it never rained. And yet he had faith in what You asked him to do and trusted You. He walked faithfully with You and this resulted in his family being saved.

Empower me to trust You in a deeper way today, Lord. Help me to walk faithfully with You and obey You even when it doesn't make sense. Thank You for drawing me closer to You today. I love You. In Jesus' name I pray, Amen.

"Noah was a righteous man, blameless among the people of his time, and he walked faithfully with God."
- Genesis 6:9 (NIV)

"By faith Noah, being divinely warned of things not yet seen, moved with godly fear, prepared an ark for the saving of his household, by which he condemned the world and became heir of the righteousness which is according to faith."
- Hebrews 11:7 (NKJV)

Also read: Genesis 6:9-22, 7:1-24

Prayer of Faith #2:
ABRAHAM'S MOVE

Lord, there are so many uncertainties in life, twists and turns on this journey of faith with You. Sometimes it is difficult to know what step to take next. I am thankful I can depend on You. You never change and are the same yesterday, today and forever.

When You asked Abraham to leave his home, You didn't tell him where he was going. It must have been difficult for him to leave his comfort zone and his family. However, he put his faith in You and took that first step of faith into the unknown. And You blessed him in many ways.

Lord, help me to be willing to step out in faith when You ask me. Help me to trust the unknown to You. You know the way and You will lead me one step at a time to my destination as I put my full trust in You.

Thank you for leading me down the path that I should go today. Amen.

"Jesus Christ is the same yesterday and today and forever."
- Hebrews 13:8 (ESV)

"Now the Lord said to Abram, 'Go from your country and your kindred and your father's house to the land that I will show you. And I will make of you a great nation, and I will bless you and make your name great, so that you will be a blessing. I will bless those who bless you, and him who dishonors you I will curse, and in you all the families of the earth shall be blessed.' So Abram went, as the Lord had told him, and Lot went with him. Abram was seventy-five years old when he departed from Haran."
- Genesis 12:1-4 (ESV)

"By faith Abraham obeyed when he was called to go out to the place which he would receive as an inheritance. And he went out, not knowing where he was going. By faith he dwelt in the land of promise as in a foreign country, dwelling in tents with Isaac and Jacob, the heirs with him of the same promise; for he waited for the city which has foundations, whose builder and maker is God."
- Hebrews 11:8-10 (NKJV)

Prayer of Faith #3:
ABRAHAM'S SON

Lord, thank You for all of Your promises to me in the Bible. Your Word is like a big treasure chest of promises from You. But I admit that sometimes it is hard for me to believe these promises are truly meant for me. Help me to overcome my unbelief and have faith in what You have promised me.

When You promised Abraham that he would be the father of many nations, he believed You. I am so thankful that being a person of faith does not equal perfection. Even when we fail You, You never fail us. And even though Abraham was not perfect in his journey of faith, Your Word says that he did not waver through unbelief regarding Your promise of having a son. And he and Sarah did have a son, Isaac, in their old age.

Strengthen my faith today where I am weak. Help me to believe Your promises for me and to live according to Your Word, not my feelings. I love You so much. Thank you for continuing to work in my life. Amen.

"If we are faithless, He remains faithful - for He cannot deny Himself."
- 2 Timothy 2:13 (ESV)

"This is my covenant with you: I will make you the father of a multitude of nations! What's more, I am changing your name. It will no longer be Abram. Instead, you will be called Abraham, for you will be the father of many nations. I will make you extremely fruitful. Your descendants will become many nations, and kings will be among them!
- Genesis 17:4-6 (NLT)

"Without weakening in his faith, he (Abraham) faced the fact that his body was as good as dead—since he was about a hundred years old—and that Sarah's womb was also dead. Yet he did not waver through unbelief regarding the promise of God, but was strengthened in his faith and gave glory to God, being fully persuaded that God had power to do what he had promised. This is why 'it was credited to him as righteousness.'"
- Romans 4:19-22 (NIV)

Prayer of Faith #4:
ABRAHAM'S SACRIFICE

Lord, living a life of faith is not always easy. Sometimes it requires a sacrifice of my time, money and/or relationships. If You ask me to give something up, it is for a purpose. Also, help me to realize that when You ask me to sacrifice something, it is for my good. You want to be first in my life, but so often I have put other idols before You. Please forgive me. I specifically confess that I often put _____ (fill in the blank) before You. Please forgive me and help me to love You with ALL my heart, soul, mind and strength.

When you asked Abraham to sacrifice his son, the son that was going to fulfill Your promise to him, he obeyed. He believed that You could raise Isaac up from the dead in order to still fulfill Your promise. Wow... what faith! You tested Abraham and he showed by his obedience that You were first in his heart...not his son. And You stopped him from harming Isaac and provided a ram for the offering instead.

Thank You, Lord, for this vivid example of faith. Strengthen my faith in You today and may I continue to put You first in my life above anyone or anything else. In Jesus' name I pray, Amen.

"And one of the scribes came up and heard them disputing with one another, and seeing that he answered them well, asked him, 'Which commandment is the most important of all?' Jesus answered, 'The most important is, 'Hear, O Israel: The Lord our God, the Lord is one. And you shall love the Lord your God with all your heart and with all your soul and with all your mind and with all your strength.'"
- Mark 12:28-30 (ESV)

"Now it came to pass after these things that God tested Abraham, and said to him, 'Abraham!' And he said, 'Here I am.' Then He said, 'Take now your son, your only son Isaac, whom you love, and go to the land of Moriah, and offer him there as a burnt offering on one of the mountains of which I shall tell you.'"
- Genesis 22:1-2 (NKJV)

"And He said, 'Do not lay your hand on the lad, or do anything to him; for now I know that you fear God, since you have not withheld your son, your only son, from Me.' Then Abraham lifted his eyes and looked, and there behind him was a ram caught in a thicket by its horns. So Abraham went and took the ram, and offered it up for a burnt offering instead of his son. And Abraham called the name of the place, The-Lord-Will Provide; as it is said to this day, 'In the Mount of the Lord it shall be provided.'"
- Genesis 22:12-14 (NKJV)

"By faith Abraham, when he was tested, offered up Isaac, and he who had received the promises offered up his only begotten son, of whom it was said, 'In Isaac your seed shall be called,' concluding that God was able to raise him up, even from the dead, from which he also received him in a figurative sense."
- Hebrews 11:17-19 (NKJV)

Also read: Entire chapter of Genesis 22

Prayer of Faith #5:
DAVID AND GOLIATH

Lord, some days my circumstances threaten to overwhelm me. It is on those days when I am tempted to worry and feel defeated. However, I know that I am never alone. You are always with me and are my strength and my provider. Help me to remember to set my mind on You and not on my circumstances.

David literally faced a giant in battle...Goliath. All the odds were against him, but he chose to trust in You. David learned to keep his eyes fixed on You and not on his circumstances. And You gave him a great victory.

Empower me to have faith like David today. A faith that trusts in Your power and not my own. A faith that knows that You are greater than any "giants" I face today. My story may end differently than David's did, but I choose to trust my circumstances to You today. Thank you for the victory You will grant me. In Jesus' name I pray, Amen.

"Set your minds on things that are above, not on things that are on earth."
- Colossians 3:2 (ESV)

"David said to the Philistine, 'You come against me with sword and spear and javelin, but I come against you in the name of the Lord Almighty, the God of the armies of Israel, whom you have defied. This day the Lord will deliver you into my hands, and I'll strike you down and cut off your head. This very day I will give the carcasses of the Philistine army to the birds and the wild animals, and the whole world will know that there is a God in Israel. All those gathered here will know that it is not by sword or spear that the Lord saves; for the battle is the Lord's, and He will give all of you into our hands.'"
- I Samuel 17:45-47 (NIV)

Also read: Entire chapter of I Samuel 17

Prayer of Faith #6:
JOSHUA AND CALEB

Thank you, Lord, for all that You have given me. I am truly blessed. And yet sometimes I listen to the lies of the enemy, Satan, who causes doubt and fear to enter my mind and heart. Help me to recognize the lies of the enemy and replace them with Your Truth.

Joshua and Caleb were among the spies who went into the land that God promised to them. It was an amazing land flowing with milk and honey. However, all of the spies except for two, Joshua and Caleb, allowed their fear of the giants in the land to keep them from enjoying the blessing You had for them. Joshua and Caleb put their trust in You and had faith that You would bring them into the land. And they ended up being the only Israelites from their generation to enter the Promised Land years later.

Lord, thank You that You have not given us a spirit of fear, but of love and self-control. Your love, perfect love, drives out fear. Therefore, I ask You to remove any fear in my heart and mind today and replace it with Your peace. Thank You for Your presence with me today. Amen.

"But Joshua the son of Nun and Caleb the son of Jephunneh, who were among those who had spied out the land, tore their clothes; and they spoke to all the congregation of the children of Israel, saying: 'The land we passed through to spy out is an exceedingly good land. If the Lord delights in us, then He will bring us into this land and give it to us, 'a land which flows with milk and honey.' Only do not rebel against the Lord, nor fear the people of the land, for they are our bread; their protection has departed from them, and the Lord is with us. Do not fear them.'"
- Numbers 14:6-9 (NKJV)

"'Of all those I rescued from Egypt, no one who is twenty years old or older will ever see the land I swore to give to Abraham, Isaac, and Jacob, for they have not obeyed me wholeheartedly. The only exceptions are Caleb son of Jephunneh the Kenizzite and Joshua son of Nun, for they have wholeheartedly followed the Lord.'"

- Numbers 32:11-12 (NLT)

"For God gave us a spirit not of fear but of power and love and self-control."
- 2 Timothy 1:7 (ESV)

"There is no fear in love, but perfect love casts out fear. For fear has to do with punishment, and whoever fears has not been perfected in love."
- 1 John 4:18 (ESV)

Also read: Numbers 13-14

Prayer of Faith #7:
QUEEN ESTHER

Lord, thank You for another day of life. You are the One who gives breath to my lungs. You also know all the days ordained for me as they have been written in Your book.

I know that You have created me for a purpose, and that purpose is to glorify You. Just as You placed Queen Esther in the king's household "for such a time as this" to save her people, You also have plans and purposes for my life. Queen Esther was willing to risk her life to come before the King on behalf of the Jewish people. I ask that You empower me today with courage through Your Holy Spirit to take risks for You. I come to you with a surrendered heart, Lord. May Your will be done in my life.

I love You so much. Amen.

"Your eyes saw my unformed body; all the days ordained for me were written in Your book before one of them came to be."
- Psalm 139:16 (NIV)

"When Esther's words were reported to Mordecai, he sent back this answer: 'Do not think that because you are in the king's house you alone of all the Jews will escape. For if you remain silent at this time, relief and deliverance for the Jews will arise from another place, but you and your father's family will perish. And who knows but that you have come to your royal position for such a time as this?' Then Esther sent this reply to Mordecai: 'Go, gather together all the Jews who are in Susa, and fast for me. Do not eat or drink for three days, night or day. I and my attendants will fast as you do. When this is done, I will go to the king, even though it is against the law. And if I perish, I perish.'"
- Esther 4:12-16 (NIV)

"Then Esther went again before the king, falling down at his feet and begging him with tears to stop the evil plot devised by Haman the Agagite against the Jews. Again the king held out the gold scepter to Esther. So she rose and stood before him. Esther said, 'If it please the king, and if I have found favor with him, and if he thinks it is right, and if I am pleasing to him, let there be a decree that reverses the orders of Haman son of Hammedatha the Agagite, who ordered that Jews throughout all the king's provinces should be destroyed. For how can I endure to see my people and my family slaughtered and destroyed?'

"Then King Xerxes said to Queen Esther and Mordecai the Jew, 'I have given Esther the property of Haman, and he has been impaled on a pole because he tried to destroy the Jews. Now go ahead and send a message to the Jews in the king's name, telling them whatever you want, and seal it with the king's signet ring. But remember that whatever has already been written in the king's name and sealed with his signet ring can never be revoked.'"
- Esther 8:3-8 (NLT)

Also read: Book of Esther

Prayer of Faith #8:
SHADRACH, MESHACH, & ABED-NEGO

Lord, there are so many things in this world that compete for my time, attention and worship. It is so easy to get caught up in worldly pursuits instead of spending time worshipping You. Please forgive me for neglecting my relationship with You. I truly do want to put You first in my life.

Empower me to take a stand in my culture like Shadrach, Meshach, and Abed-Nego did. Instead of bowing down and worshipping the golden image of Nebuchadnezzar, they took a stand for You. They declared that You were able to deliver them from the fiery furnace, but even if You did not, they would not compromise their beliefs. Wow. And You did deliver them from the furnace and rewarded them for their obedience to You.

No matter what the outcome may be, Lord, grant me a willingness to obey You. Strengthen my faith in You. Thank You for opening my eyes to Your Truth and drawing me to Yourself. I pray that I would stand strong in Your strength and not my own strength when my faith is challenged. In Jesus' name I pray, Amen.

"Then Nebuchadnezzar, in rage and fury, gave the command to bring Shadrach, Meshach, and Abed-Nego. So they brought these men before the king. Nebuchadnezzar spoke, saying to them, 'Is it true, Shadrach, Meshach, and Abed-Nego, that you do not serve my gods or worship the gold image which I have set up? Now if you are ready at the time you hear the sound of the horn, flute, harp, lyre, and psaltery, in symphony with all kinds of music, and you fall down and worship the image which I have made, good! But if you do not worship, you shall be cast immediately into the midst of a burning fiery furnace. And who is the god who will deliver you from my hands?'

Shadrach, Meshach, and Abed-Nego answered and said to the king, 'O Nebuchadnezzar, we have no need to answer you in this matter. If that is the case, our God whom we serve is able to deliver us from the burning fiery furnace, and He will deliver us from your hand, O king. But if not, let it be known to you, O king, that we do not serve your gods, nor will we worship the gold image which you have set up.'

... 'Look!' he answered, 'I see four men loose, walking in the midst of the fire; and they are not hurt, and the form of the fourth is like the Son of God.' Then Nebuchadnezzar went near the mouth of the burning fiery furnace and spoke, saying, 'Shadrach, Meshach, and Abed-Nego, servants of the Most High God, come out, and come here.' Then Shadrach, Meshach, and Abed-Nego came from the midst of the fire."
- Daniel 3:13-18, 25-26 (NKJV)

Also read: Entire chapter of Daniel 3

Prayer of Faith 9:
DANIEL

Lord, thank You for strengthening my faith in You. You are not a distant God, but instead, You desire a personal relationship with me. May our relationship continue to grow deeper with each passing day. Increase my love for You today.

Daniel had an unwavering faith in You. Even when his life was at risk, he still took the time to pray to You. His enemies came against him, but You spared his life when he was thrown into the lion's den. Why? Because he trusted in You.

Protect me from my enemies today in Jesus' name. May You be glorified in everything I do and say. And may my life demonstrate my deep trust in You. I love You so much. Amen.

"Then Daniel said to the king, 'O king, live forever! My God sent his angel and shut the lions' mouths, and they have not harmed me, because I was found blameless before Him; and also before you, O king, I have done no harm.' Then the king was exceedingly glad, and commanded that Daniel be taken up out of the den. So Daniel was taken up out of the den, and no kind of harm was found on him, because he had trusted in his God."

- Daniel 6:21-23 (ESV)

Also read: Entire chapter of Daniel 6

Prayer of Faith #10: WOMAN HEALED

I feel desperate for you today, Lord. I am hard pressed on every side, but not crushed; perplexed but not in despair; struck down, but not destroyed. And yet I know You are with me through every dark trial that I walk through.

Like the woman who had been bleeding for 12 years and was desperate to be healed, I am desperate for You. She knew that You had the power to heal her and she believed that if she simply touched the hem of Your garment, she would be healed. And she was healed. Instantly. You said her faith made her well.

And so today I reach out for You. I know that no one else has the answers or the ability to heal me but You. You are the Alpha and Omega; the Beginning and the

End.   I thank You for giving me the faith to simply reach for You. May You bring healing to me today where I need it. I pray all this in Jesus' name, Amen.

"We are hard pressed on every side, but not crushed; perplexed, but not in despair; persecuted, but not abandoned; struck down, but not destroyed."
- 2 Corinthians 4:8-9 (NIV)

"As Jesus went, the people pressed around him. And there was a woman who had had a discharge of blood for twelve years, and though she had spent all her living on physicians, she could not be healed by anyone. She came up behind him and touched the fringe of his garment, and immediately her discharge of blood ceased. And Jesus said, 'Who was it that touched me?' When all denied it, Peter said, 'Master, the crowds surround you and are pressing in on you!' But Jesus said, 'Someone touched me, for I perceive that power has gone out from me.' And when the woman saw that she was not hidden, she came trembling, and falling down before him declared in the presence of all the people why she had touched him, and how she had been immediately healed. And he said to her, 'Daughter, your faith has made you well; go in peace.'"
- Luke 4:42-48 (ESV)

"I am the Alpha and the Omega, the First and the Last, the Beginning and the End."

- Revelation 22:13 (NLT)

Prayer of Faith #11:
BLIND MEN

Lord, sometimes I simply need to ask You for what I need instead of worrying or complaining. Increase my faith in Your ability to meet my needs just like the blind men sitting along the roadside that came to You with their need and told You specifically what they wanted. They wanted their sight and You chose to heal them that day.

Your Word says we do not have because we have not asked You. Therefore, today I come to You asking You for what I need - _____ (insert your request here).

Help me to put my trust in You and not my own self-sufficiency. Empower me to depend on You and come to You first asking for what I need before I go to others or try to figure it out myself. I love You Lord, Amen.

"As Jesus and his disciples were leaving Jericho, a large crowd followed him. Two blind men were sitting by the roadside, and when they heard that Jesus was going by, they shouted, 'Lord, Son of David, have mercy on us!' The crowd rebuked them and told them to be quiet, but they shouted all the louder, 'Lord, Son of David, have mercy on us!' Jesus stopped and called them. 'What do you want me to do for you?' he asked. 'Lord,' they answered, 'we want our sight.' Jesus had compassion on them and touched their eyes. Immediately they received their sight and followed him."
- Matthew 20:29-34 (NIV)

"You do not have because you do not ask God."
- James 4:2b (NIV)

Prayer of Faith #12:
BOY'S FATHER

Lord, I thank You for another day. Although this life is full of challenges and difficulties I know that the one constant in my life is You. You have promised to never leave me or forsake me.

Sometimes when I'm faced with a trial, my faith wavers. Similar to the boy's father who said "IF you can do anything have compassion on us and help us," I sometimes doubt You. I need to be reminded of the response You gave that boy's father that day...

"If you can! All things are possible for one who believes."

Even though You may not choose to answer my prayers in the ways I would like them to be answered,

You always have the power to do above and beyond anything that I can think or imagine.

And so today, I pray the same prayer that father prayed...Lord, I do believe; help my unbelief! Thank You for continuing to do Your work in my heart and my life. Amen.

"Never will I leave you; never will I forsake you."
- Hebrews 13:5 (NIV)

"And Jesus asked his father, 'How long has this been happening to him?" And he said, "From childhood. And it has often cast him into fire and into water, to destroy him. But if you can do anything, have compassion on us and help us.' And Jesus said to him, 'If you can! All things are possible for one who believes.' Immediately the father of the child cried out and said, 'I believe; help my unbelief!' And when Jesus saw that a crowd came running together, he rebuked the unclean spirit, saying to it, 'You mute and deaf spirit, I command you, come out of him and never enter him again.' And after crying out and convulsing him terribly, it came out, and the boy was like a corpse, so that most of them said, 'He is dead.' But Jesus took him by the hand and lifted him up, and he arose."
- Mark 9:21-27 (ESV)

"Now to him who is able to do immeasurably more than all we ask or imagine, according to his power that is at work within us, to him be glory in the church and in Christ Jesus throughout all generations, for ever and ever! Amen."

- Ephesians 3:20-21 (NIV)

Prayer of Faith #13: CENTURION

Jesus, as I read about Your life in the Bible, I grow to know You better. One of the things You looked for and commended in people was their faith. In fact, Your Word tells us that without faith it is impossible to please You.

There was a centurion who came to You and asked You to heal his servant. He knew that You had the authority to heal his servant even at a distance. Just like the centurion would command those under his authority to do something and they would do it, he believed You could simply say the Word and in the authority given to You by God, his servant would be healed. And his servant was healed that very hour.

Lord, help to expand my faith in You today. Give me faith like this centurion to believe that Your authority has no boundaries. Remove any doubt in my mind and my heart today in Jesus' name. Amen.

"And without faith it is impossible to please Him, for whoever would draw near to God must believe that He exists and that He rewards those who seek Him."
- Hebrews 11:6 (ESV)

"Now when Jesus had entered Capernaum, a centurion came to Him, pleading with Him, saying, 'Lord, my servant is lying at home paralyzed, dreadfully tormented.' And Jesus said to him, 'I will come and heal him.' The centurion answered and said, 'Lord, I am not worthy that You should come under my roof. But only speak a word, and my servant will be healed. For I also am a man under authority, having soldiers under me. And I say to this one, 'Go,' and he goes; and to another, 'Come,' and he comes; and to my servant, 'Do this,' and he does it.' When Jesus heard it, He marveled, and said to those who followed, 'Assuredly, I say to you, I have not found such great faith, not even in Israel! And I say to you that many will come from east and west, and sit down with Abraham, Isaac, and Jacob in the kingdom of heaven. But the sons of the kingdom will be cast out into outer darkness. There will be weeping and gnashing of teeth.' Then Jesus said to the centurion, 'Go your way; and as you have believed, so let it be done for you.' And his servant was healed that same hour."

- Matthew 8:5-13 (NKJV)

Prayer of Faith #14:
MARY

Father, there are so many examples of people who lived a life of faith in the Bible. I am encouraged to know they are ordinary people just like me. I do not need to be a "super Christian" in order to have faith. I simply need You.

You chose Mary to be the mother of Your son, Jesus. When Your Angel gave her the news, Mary did have a couple questions. However, her questions were not asked from a spirit of doubt. In the end, Mary said to Your messenger, "may it be to me as you have said," indicating her surrendered heart and faith in Your plan.

Help me to surrender my life to You today. Give me the faith to trust Your plans for me. As Jesus said in the garden of Gethsemane, "not my will, but Yours, be done," May that also be my prayer today. I love You, Lord. Amen.

"In the sixth month the angel Gabriel was sent from God to a city of Galilee named Nazareth, to a virgin betrothed to a man whose name was Joseph, of the house of David. And the virgin's name was Mary. And he came to her and said, 'Greetings, O favored one, the Lord is with you!' But she was greatly troubled at the saying, and tried to discern what sort of greeting this might be. And the angel said to her, 'Do not be afraid, Mary, for you have found favor with God. And behold, you will conceive in your womb and bear a son, and you shall call his name Jesus. He will be great and will be called the Son of the Most High. And the Lord God will give to him the throne of his father David, and he will reign over the house of Jacob forever, and of his kingdom there will be no end.' And Mary said to the angel, 'How will this be, since I am a virgin?' And the angel answered her, 'The Holy Spirit will come upon you, and the power of the Most High will overshadow you; therefore the child to be born will be called holy— the Son of God. And behold, your relative Elizabeth in her old age has also conceived a son, and this is the sixth month with her who was called barren. For nothing will be impossible with God.' And Mary said, 'Behold, I

am the servant of the Lord; let it be to me according to your word." And the angel departed from her.'"
- Luke 1:26-38 (ESV)

"Father, if you are willing, remove this cup from me. Nevertheless, not my will, but Yours, be done."
- Luke 22:42 (ESV)

Prayer of Faith #15:
PARALYTIC

Lord, many days I am burdened by the needs of others. So many people are struggling with personal problems, health problems, financial issues, etc. However, I am not meant to carry their burdens alone. Instead, I am to bring them to You in faith.

The story of the paralytic illustrates this so well. He had a great need. He was paralyzed and could not walk or work. He was dependent on others. Instead of his friends taking on that burden themselves, they carried him to Jesus. Literally. And when they saw there was no way to reach Jesus because of the crowds, they did not give up. Instead, in faith, they dug a hole in the roof and lowered their friend to Jesus. Seeing their faith, Jesus forgave his sins and healed him.

Lord, I ask You today to fill me with this kind of faith for the people in my life. Instead of worrying or trying to find a solution myself, empower me to bring them to You in prayer. Then, give me faith in You to know that I can trust You with the results. Show me if there is anything You want me to do for them. But most importantly, remind me to continue to bring them to You in prayer. Remove any worry from my mind today in Jesus' name. Amen.

"When Jesus returned to Capernaum several days later, the news spread quickly that he was back home. Soon the house where he was staying was so packed with visitors that there was no more room, even outside the door. While he was preaching God's word to them, four men arrived carrying a paralyzed man on a mat. They couldn't bring him to Jesus because of the crowd, so they dug a hole through the roof above his head. Then they lowered the man on his mat, right down in front of Jesus. Seeing their faith, Jesus said to the paralyzed man, 'My child, your sins are forgiven.' But some of the teachers of religious law who were sitting there thought to themselves, 'What is he saying? This is blasphemy! Only God can forgive sins!' Jesus knew immediately what they were thinking, so he asked them, 'Why do you question this in your hearts? Is it easier to say to the paralyzed man 'Your sins are forgiven,' or 'Stand up, pick up your mat, and walk'? So I will prove to you that the Son of Man has the authority on earth to forgive sins.' Then Jesus turned to the paralyzed man and said, 'Stand up, pick up your mat, and go home!' And the man jumped up, grabbed his mat, and walked out through the stunned onlookers. They were all amazed and praised God, exclaiming, 'We've never seen anything like this before!'"

- Mark 2:1-12 (NLT)

Prayer of Faith #16:
JESUS' OBEDIENCE

Lord, I am so thankful for the example You have given us in Jesus. He had ultimate trust in You and faith in Your plan even when it was not what His flesh wanted. Faith leads to obedience. And I see this lived out so clearly in the life of Christ. He said He did nothing by Himself but only what He saw You, His Father, doing.

Therefore, I not only need to have faith in You but to also prove my faith in You through my obedience to Your commands. And I do not have to do this in my own strength or my own sufficiency. I can do all things through Christ who strengthens me.

Empower me to obey You even when it is difficult and hard. Help me to follow the example Christ set for me when He walked this earth. I love You so much, Lord. Amen.

"Jesus gave them this answer: 'Very truly I tell you, the Son can do nothing by himself; he can do only what he sees his Father doing, because whatever the Father does the Son also does.'"
- John 5:19 (NIV)

"I can do all things through Him who strengthens me."
- Philippians 4:13 (ESV)

Prayer of Faith 17:
SALVATION

Lord, today I want to thank You for my salvation. I know that without You, I would have no hope beyond this life. For I have sinned against You in so many ways and my sin separates me from You. Thank You that You have given me the gift of eternal life through the sacrifice Jesus made on the cross. So many misunderstand You...You did not send Jesus to condemn the world, but to save it. I pray that my unsaved relatives and friends would come to truly know You and trust in Jesus for their salvation. For when we confess with our mouths that Jesus is Lord and believe in our hearts that You raised him from the dead, we will be saved.

I thank You that salvation is truly a gift from You, nothing I can earn by doing good works or trying harder. Faith without works is dead, but ultimately salvation comes only as a gift from You.

I praise You that I am a new creation – the old has passed away and the new has come. Thank You for changing my heart and my life…I am forever grateful to You. Help me to share my relationship with You with others. Amen.

"For all have sinned and fall short of the glory of God."
~ Romans 3:23 (NKJV)

"For the wages of sin is death, but the gift of God is eternal life in Christ Jesus our Lord."
~ Romans 6:23 (NKJV)

"For God so loved the world that He gave His only begotten Son, that whoever believes in Him should not perish but have everlasting life. For God did not send His Son into the world to condemn the world, but that the world through Him might be saved."
~ John 3:16-17 (NKJV)

"That if you confess with your mouth the Lord Jesus and believe in your heart that God has raised Him from the dead, you will be saved."
~ Romans 10:9 (NKJV)

"For by grace you have been saved through faith, and that not of yourselves; it is the gift of God."
~ Ephesians 2:8 (NKJV)

"Thus also faith by itself, if it does not have works, is dead."
~ James 2:17 (NKJV)

"Therefore, if anyone is in Christ, he is a new creation; old things have passed away; behold, all things have become new."
~ 2 Corinthians 5:17 (NKJV)

Prayer of Faith #18: LOVE

Lord, I thank You that my relationship with You is not built around rules but instead is built upon love. Sometimes I get into a pattern of simply coming to You out of routine and habit. I do know that creating a habit of meeting with You is important. However, what is even more important is that my heart connects with You on a regular basis.

I can have all the faith in the world and yet if I do not have love, my faith means nothing. Therefore, today I ask You to fill me to overflowing with Your love. If there is any part of my heart that has become cold, I ask You to fill it with Your love once again. Show me Lord if there is anything blocking me from truly living a life of love. Reveal to me any unforgiveness, resentment, bitterness or hate in my heart. Right now, I confess that my heart has grown cold in this area _____ (fill in the blank). Please forgive me and wash me clean through Your forgiveness. Fill me once again with Your spirit and Your love. Thank You Lord. Amen.

"If I speak in the tongues of men and of angels, but have not love, I am a noisy gong or a clanging cymbal. And if I have prophetic powers, and understand all mysteries and all knowledge, and if I have all faith, so as to remove mountains, but have not love, I am nothing. If I give away all I have, and if I deliver up my body to be burned, but have not love, I gain nothing."
- I Corinthians 13:1-3 (ESV)

Prayer of Faith #19:
FAITH AND WORKS

Father, thank You for the ways You are growing my faith in You. I know that on this side of heaven, I will continue to have opportunities to trust You and put my faith in You.

However, Your Word tells me that faith without works is dead. In fact, even the demons believe in You and shudder. And so I want my faith in You to be more than just a belief in You. I want my faith to result in obedience to You. Help me to not only talk to You in my prayers, but to also take the time to listen to You. You speak to me clearly through Your Word and through Your Holy Spirit.

Thank You, Lord, that Your Word is a lamp unto my feet and a light unto my path. Empower me to follow

You in obedience as You lead me each day. Thank You for Your Presence that is with me every day. In Jesus' name I pray, Amen.

"What does it profit, my brethren, if someone says he has faith but does not have works? Can faith save him? If a brother or sister is naked and destitute of daily food, and one of you says to them, 'Depart in peace, be warmed and filled,' but you do not give them the things which are needed for the body, what does it profit? Thus also faith by itself, if it does not have works, is dead."
- James 2:14-17 (NKJV)

"You believe that God is one; you do well. Even the demons believe—and shudder!"
- James 2:19 (ESV)

"Your word is a lamp to my feet and a light to my path."
 - Psalm 119:105 (ESV)

Prayer of Faith #20:
GOD'S WORD

Lord, thank You for Your Word, the Bible. Through it, You speak to me, teach me, and help me to grow in my relationship with You. Strengthen my faith in Your Word today. May You help me to believe that Your Word is absolute truth. It is alive and full of power and applicable to my life today.

All Scripture has been inspired by You and I can put my trust in it. Give me a hunger and thirst for Your Word. May I see it as life-giving and necessary for my spiritual life. May Your Holy Spirit teach me through Your Word and help me to understand it and apply it to my life. I love You! Amen.

"For the Word that God speaks is alive and full of power [making it active, operative, energizing, and effective];

it is sharper than any two-edged sword, penetrating to the dividing line of the breath of life (soul) and [the immortal] spirit, and of joints and marrow [of the deepest parts of our nature], exposing and sifting and analyzing and judging the very thoughts and purposes of the heart."
 - Hebrews 4:12 (AMP)

"Every Scripture is God-breathed (given by His inspiration) and profitable for instruction, for reproof and conviction of sin, for correction of error and discipline in obedience, [and] for training in righteousness (in holy living, in conformity to God's will in thought, purpose, and action)."
 - 2 Timothy 3:16 (AMP)

Prayer of Faith #21:
PLEASING GOD

Lord, I want to please You with my life. I know that Your Word says that without faith it is impossible to please You. Therefore, I desire to continue to grow in my faith in You each day. My faith is similar to a muscle. The more I use it, the more it grows. However, I am so thankful that it is not up to me to increase my faith. I am so thankful that You are the author and the perfecter of my faith. When my faith feels weak or wavers, I simply need to come to You and ask You for help.

Thank You for all that You are doing in my life, Lord. Help me to keep my eyes fixed on You and not on my circumstances or on myself. I love You so much. In Jesus' name I pray, Amen.

"And without faith it is impossible to please God, because anyone who comes to him must believe that he exists and that he rewards those who earnestly seek him."

 - Hebrews 11:6 (NIV)

"Therefore, since we are surrounded by so great a cloud of witnesses, let us also lay aside every weight, and sin which clings so closely, and let us run with endurance the race that is set before us, looking to Jesus, the founder and perfecter of our faith, who for the joy that was set before him endured the cross, despising the shame, and is seated at the right hand of the throne of God."

 - Hebrews 12:1-2 (ESV)

CJ AND SHELLEY HITZ

CJ and Shelley Hitz enjoy sharing God's Truth through their speaking engagements and their writing. On downtime, they enjoy spending time outdoors running, hiking and exploring God's beautiful creation.

To find out more about their ministry or to invite them to your next event, check out their website:

www.ShelleyHitz.com

Note from the Author: Reviews are gold to authors! If you have enjoyed this book, would you consider reviewing it on Amazon.com? Thank you!

OTHER RESOURCES FROM SHELLEY HITZ

For Writing: Shelley is an author coach and has many resources for writers and authors.

Writing Week: a free 7-day writing challenge. Get started here: www.writingweek.com

Free Training: get all her free training for authors here: www.trainingauthors.com/free

For Creativity: Shelley is an artist and teaches online art classes.

Get started with three free classes here: www.yourcreativeadventure.com/free